# 2016 Calendar – Japan Outdoor Photos – U.S.A. Version

## (United States National Holidays Shown)
## (Full Moon Dates = ☺ )

## Copyright © 2015 Daniel H. Wieczorek & Kazuya Numazawa

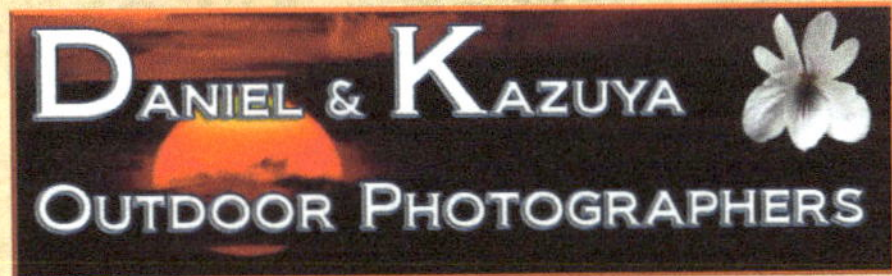





ISBN-10: 0996362673
ISBN-13: 978-0-9963626-7-2


## PHOTOS INCLUDED IN THIS CALENDAR

**January:** An Ice Covered Hyakuhiro Waterfall.  Western Tokyo, Japan.
**February:** A Beautiful Plum Tree at Kyodo-No- Mori Park.  Fuchu City, Tokyo, Japan.
**March:** The Hakuba Mountains, from Tsugaike Kogen.  Nagano Prefecture, Japan.
**April:** A Beautiful Cherry Tree in a Yard in the Foothills.  Western Tokyo, Japan.
**May:** A Heavily Manipulated Photo of Mt. Fuji.  Western Tokyo, Japan.
**June:** An Extremely Rare *Paeonia obovata* Found in a Secret Location.  Eastern Japan.
**July:** Mt. Fuji, Taken from Kawaguchi Lake Station.  Yamanashi Prefecture, Japan.
**August:** Mt. Hiuchigatake & Oze Marsh, Oze National Park.  Fukushima Prefecture, Japan.
**September:** Mt. Chokai & Interesting Cloud Phenomenon.  Yamagata/Akita Prefectures, Japan.
**October:** Mt. Fuji from the Okuniwa Area.  Yamanashi Prefecture, Japan.
**November:** A Beautiful Red Maple at Jindai Botanical Garden.  Tokyo, Japan.
**December:** "Diamond Fuji" – The Day the Sun Sets Behind Mt. Fuji – Taken at Summit of Mt. Takao.  Tokyo, Japan.

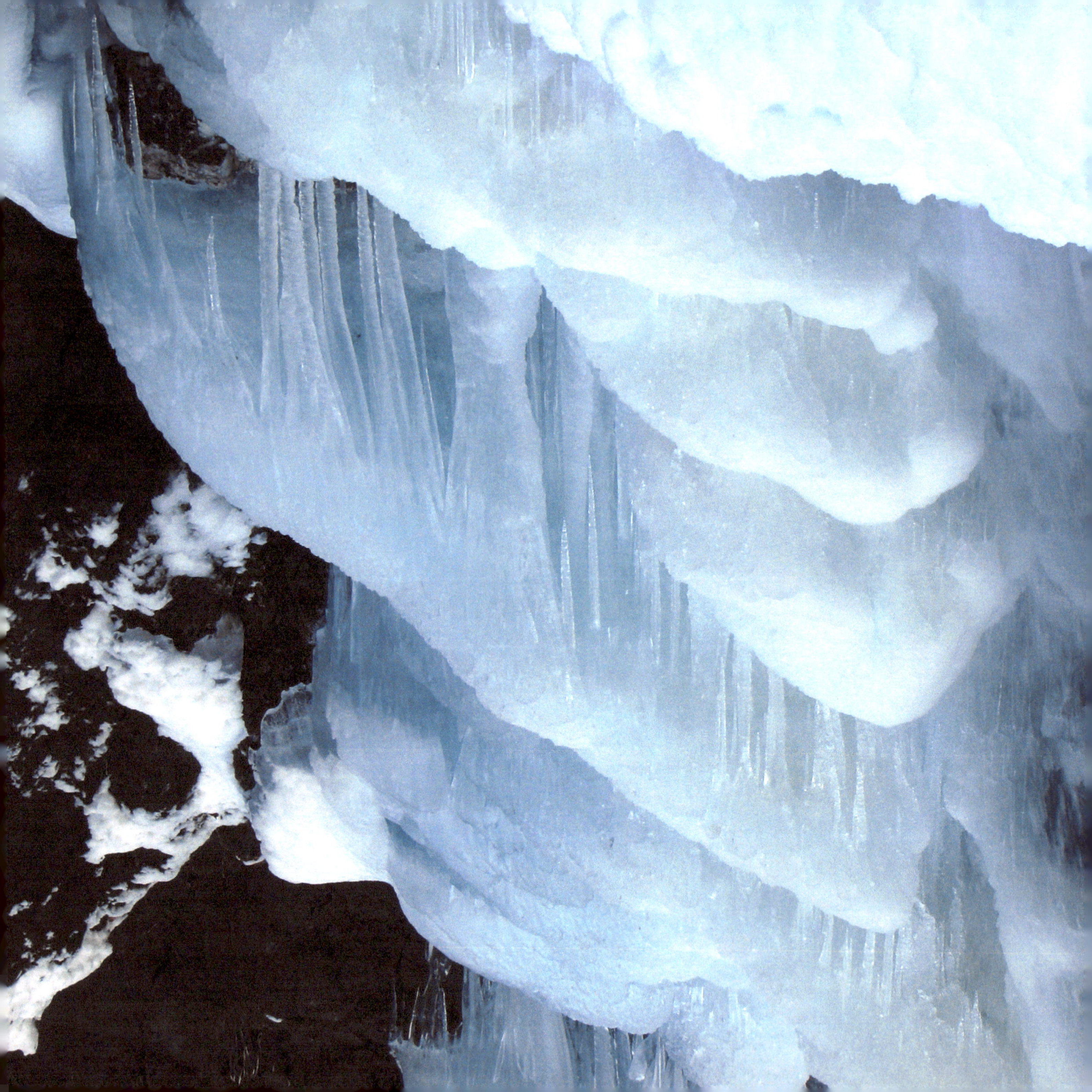

# January

## 2016

| Sun | Mon | Tue | Wed | Thu | Fri | Sat |
|---|---|---|---|---|---|---|
| 27 | 28 | 29 | 30 | 31 | 1<br>New Year's Day | 2 |
| 3 | 4 | 5 | 6 | 7 | 8 | 9 |
| 10 | 11 | 12 | 13 | 14 | 15 | 16 |
| 17 | 18<br>Martin Luther King Day | 19 | 20 | 21 | 22 | |
| 24 | 25 | 26 | 27 | 28 | 29 | 30 |
| 31 | 1 | 2 | 3 | 4 | 5 | 6 |

An Ice Covered Hyakuhiro Waterfall.  Western Tokyo, Japan.

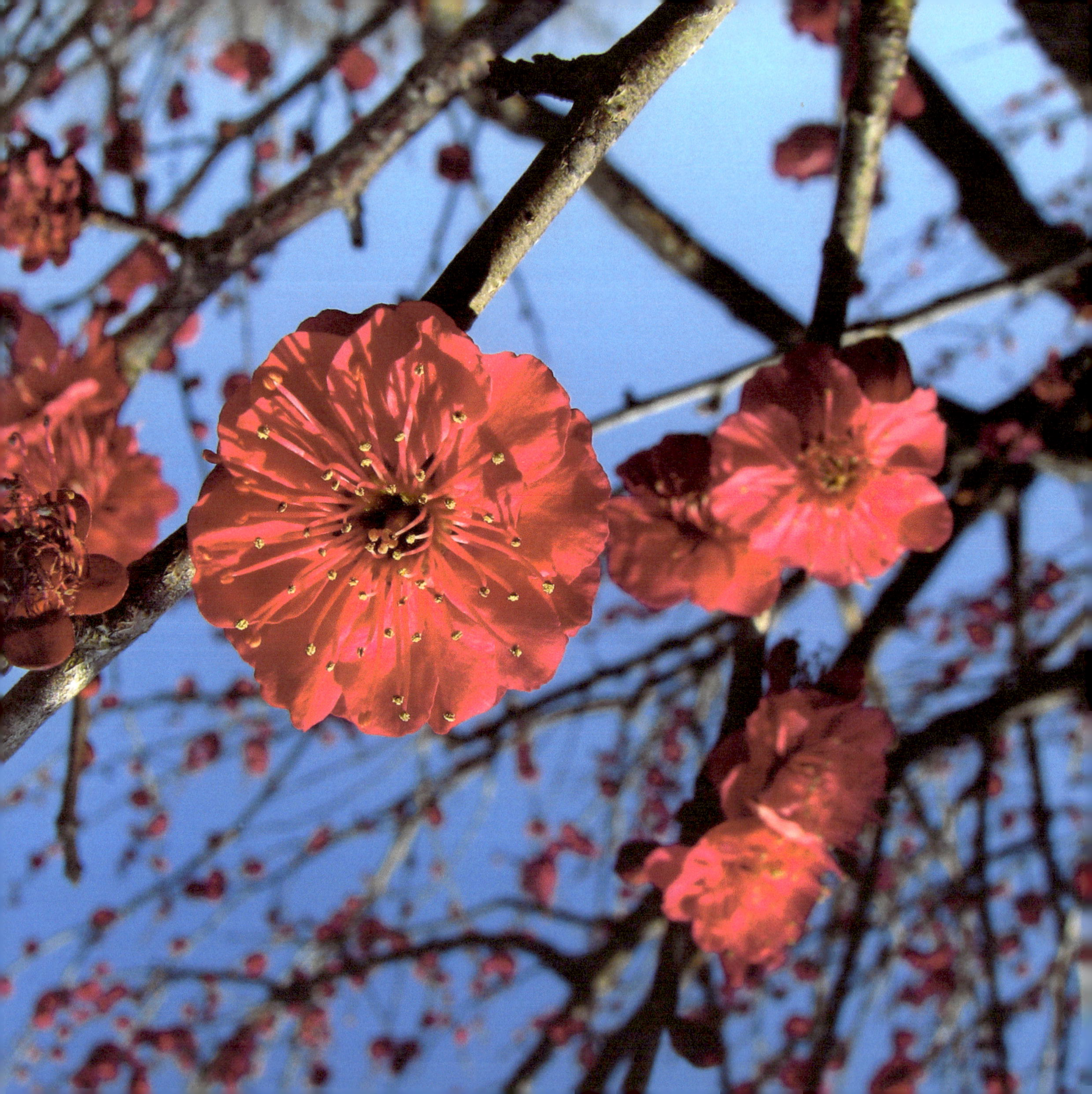

# February 2016

| Sun | Mon | Tue | Wed | Thu | Fri | Sat |
|-----|-----|-----|-----|-----|-----|-----|
| 31 | 1 | 2 | 3 | 4 | 5 | 6 |
| 7 | 8 | 9 | 10 | 11 | 12 | 13 |
| 14<br>Valentine's Day | 15<br>President's Day | 16 | 17 | 18 | 19 | 20 |
| 21 | ☻ | 23 | 24 | 25 | 26 | 27 |
| 28 | 29 | 1 | 2 | 3 | 4 | 5 |

A Beautiful Plum Tree at Kyodo-No- Mori Park.  Fuchu City, Tokyo, Japan.

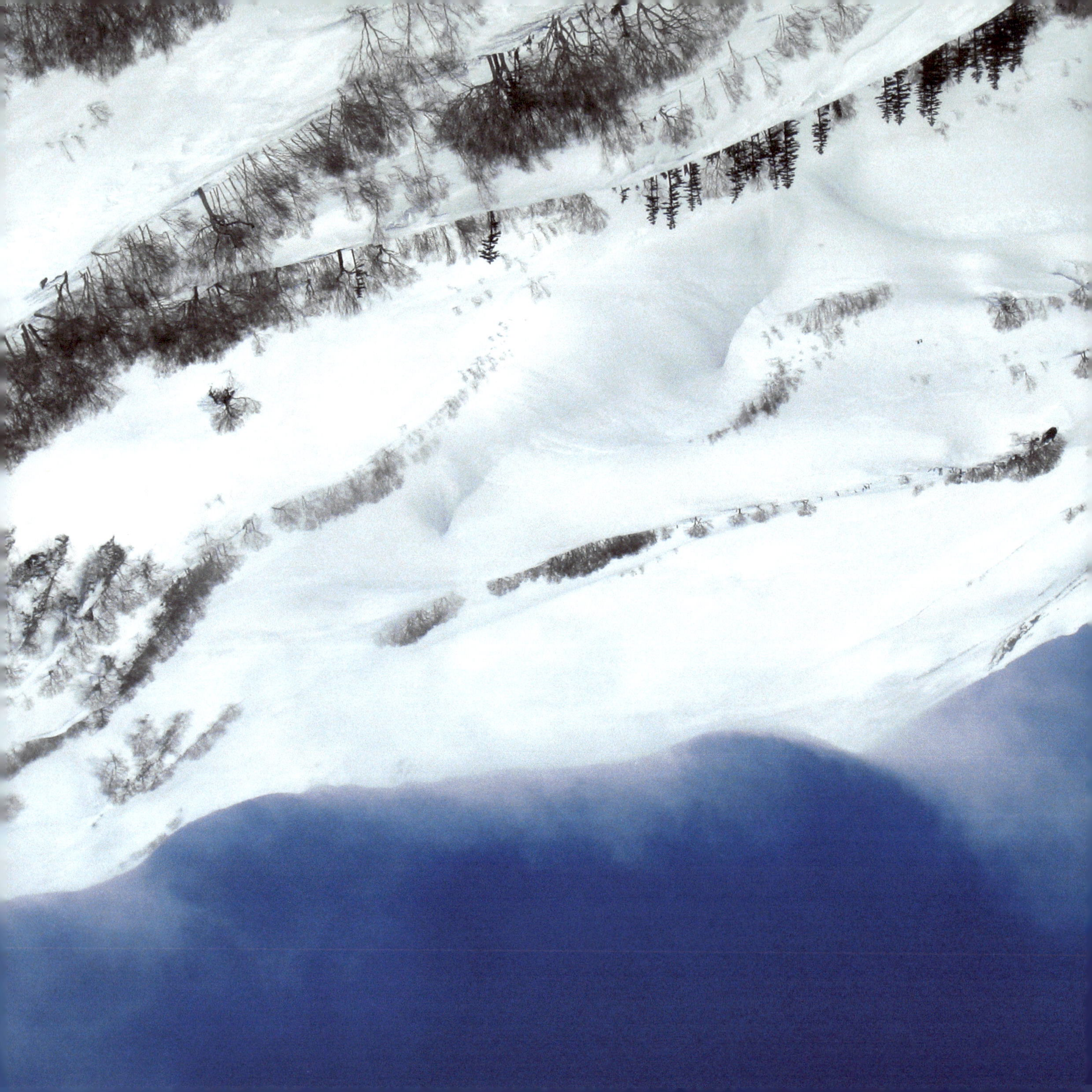

# March 2016

| Sun | Mon | Tue | Wed | Thu | Fri | Sat |
|---|---|---|---|---|---|---|
| 28 | 29 | 1 | 2 | 3 | 4 | 5 |
| 6 | 7 | 8 | 9 | 10 | 11 | 12 |
| 13 | 14 | 15 | 16 | 17 | 18 | 19 |
| 20 | 21 | 22 | 🌚 | 24 | 25 | 26 |
| 27 | 28 | 29 | 30 | 31 | 1 | 2 |

**13** — Daylight Saving Time Begin (02:00)

**20** — 04:30 GMT Vernal Equinox

**27** — Easter Sunday

The Hakuba Mountains, from Tsugaike Kogen.  Nagano Prefecture, Japan.

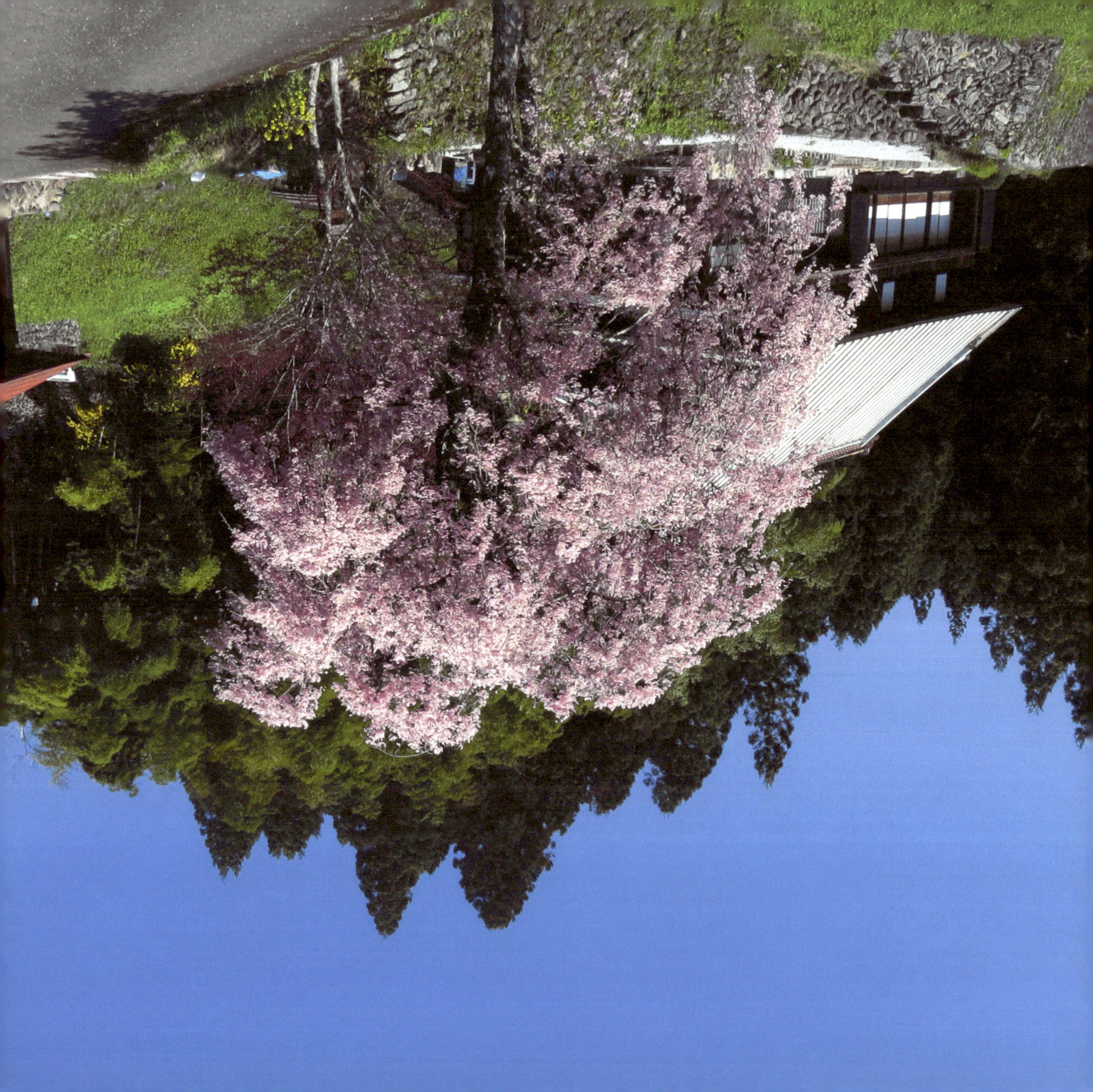

# April 2016

| Sun | Mon | Tue | Wed | Thu | Fri | Sat |
|---|---|---|---|---|---|---|
| 27 | 28 | 29 | 30 | 31 | 1 | 2 |
| 3 | 4 | 5 | 6 | 7 | 8 | 9 |
| 10 | 11 | 12 | 13 | 14 | 15 | 16 |
| 17 | 18 | 19 | 20 | 21 | ☺ | 23 |
| 24 | 25 | 26 | 27 | 28 | 29 | 30 |

A Beautiful Cherry Tree in a Yard in the Foothills.  Western Tokyo, Japan.

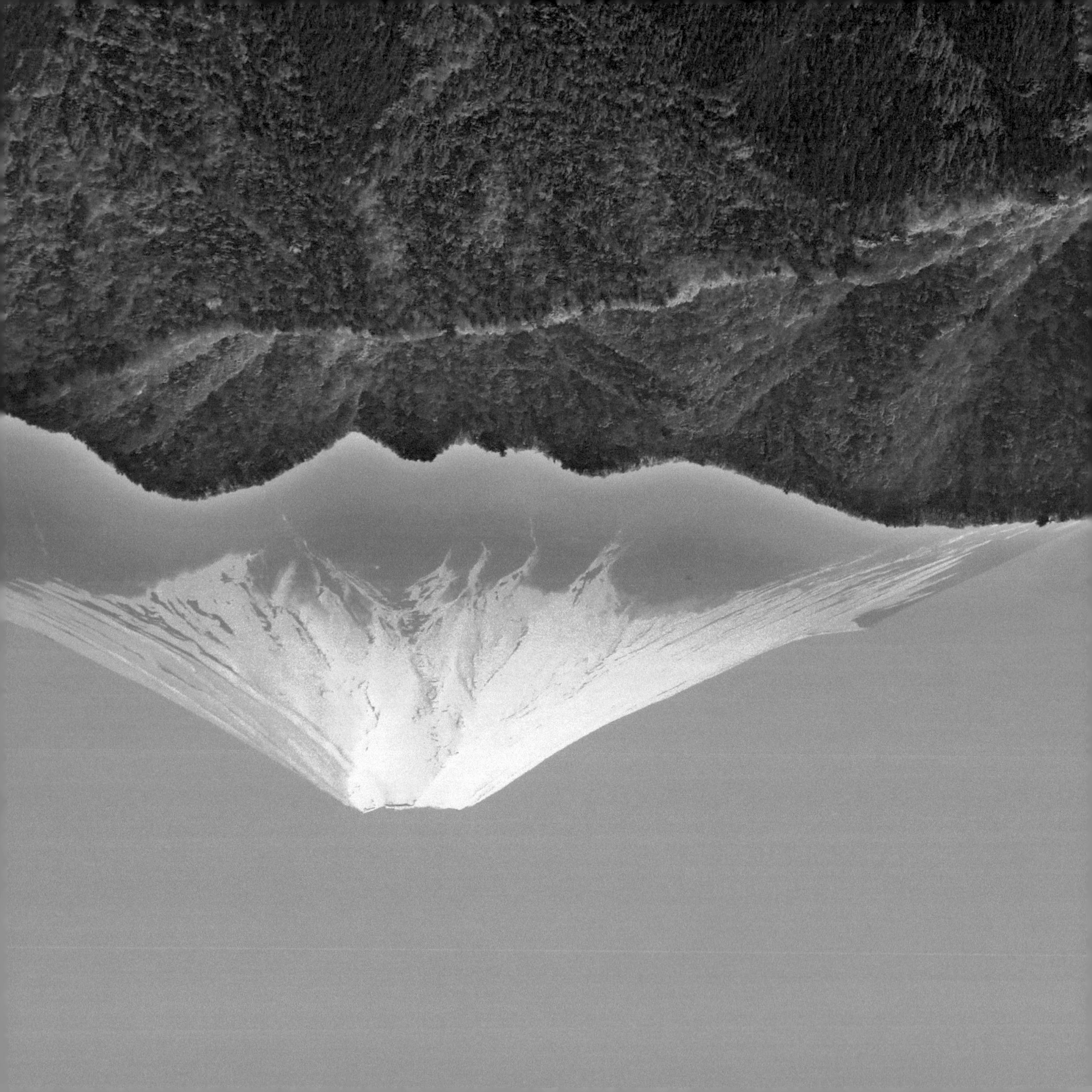

# May 2016

| Sun | Mon | Tue | Wed | Thu | Fri | Sat |
|---|---|---|---|---|---|---|
| 1 | 2 | 3 | 4 | 5 | 6 | 7 |
| 8<br>Mothers' Day | 9 | 10 | 11 | 12 | 13 | 14 |
| 15 | 16 | 17 | 18 | 19 | 20 | |
| 22 | 23 | 24 | 25 | 26 | 27 | 28 |
| 29 | 30<br>Memorial Day | 31 | 1 | 2 | 3 | 4 |

A Heavily Manipulated Photo of Mt. Fuji.  Western Tokyo, Japan.

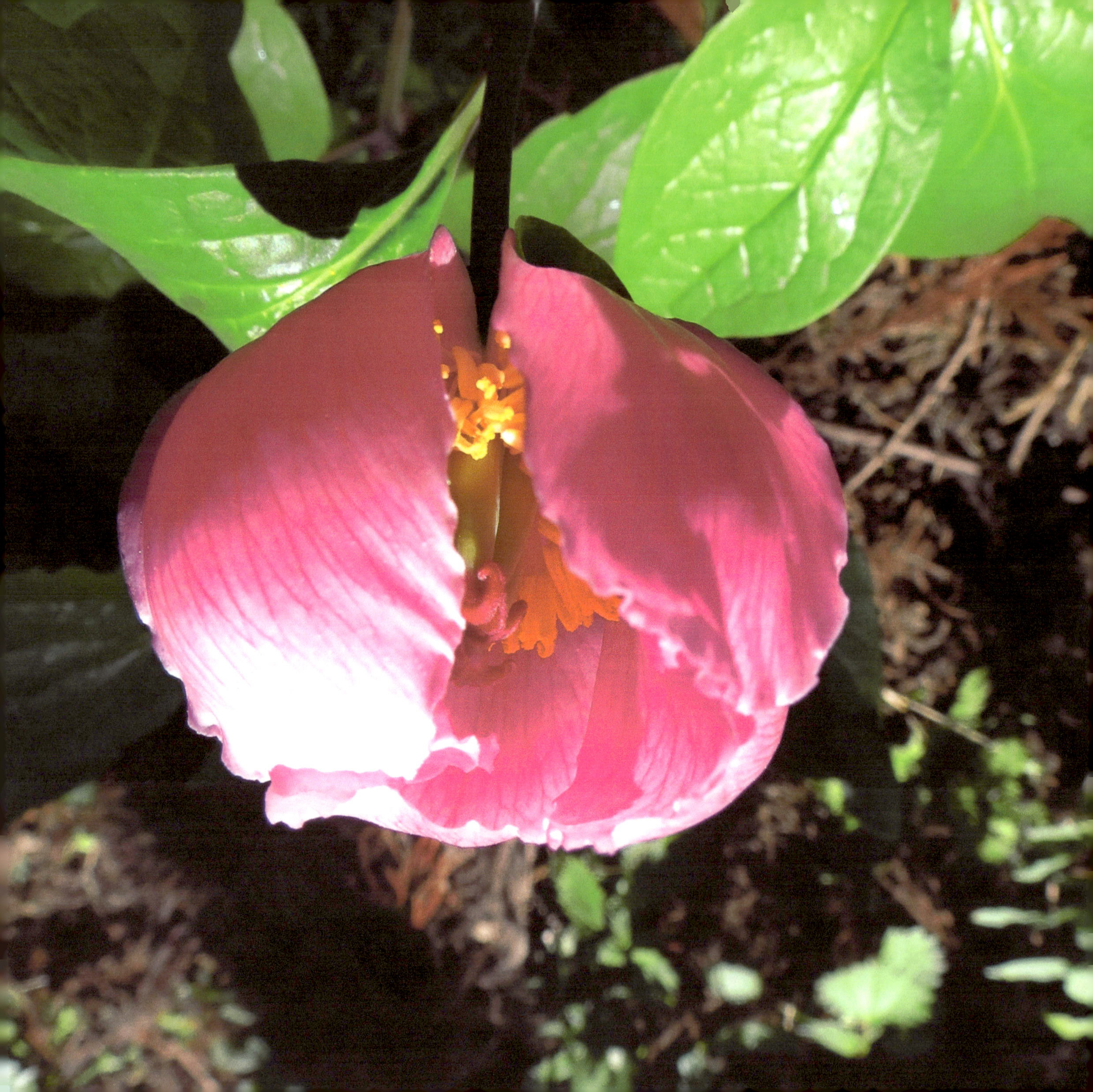

| Sun | Mon | Tue | Wed | Thu | Fri | Sat |
|-----|-----|-----|-----|-----|-----|-----|
| 29 | 30 | 31 | 1 | 2 | 3 | 4 |
| 5 | 6 | 7 | 8 | 9 | 10 | 11 |
| 12 | 13 | 14 | 15 | 16 | 17 | 18 |
| 19<br>Fathers' Day | ☻<br>22:34 GMT<br>Summer Solstice | 21 | 22 | 23 | 24 | 25 |
| 26 | 27 | 28 | 29 | 30 | 1 | 2 |

An Extremely Rare *Paeonia obovata* Found in a Secret Location.  Eastern Japan.

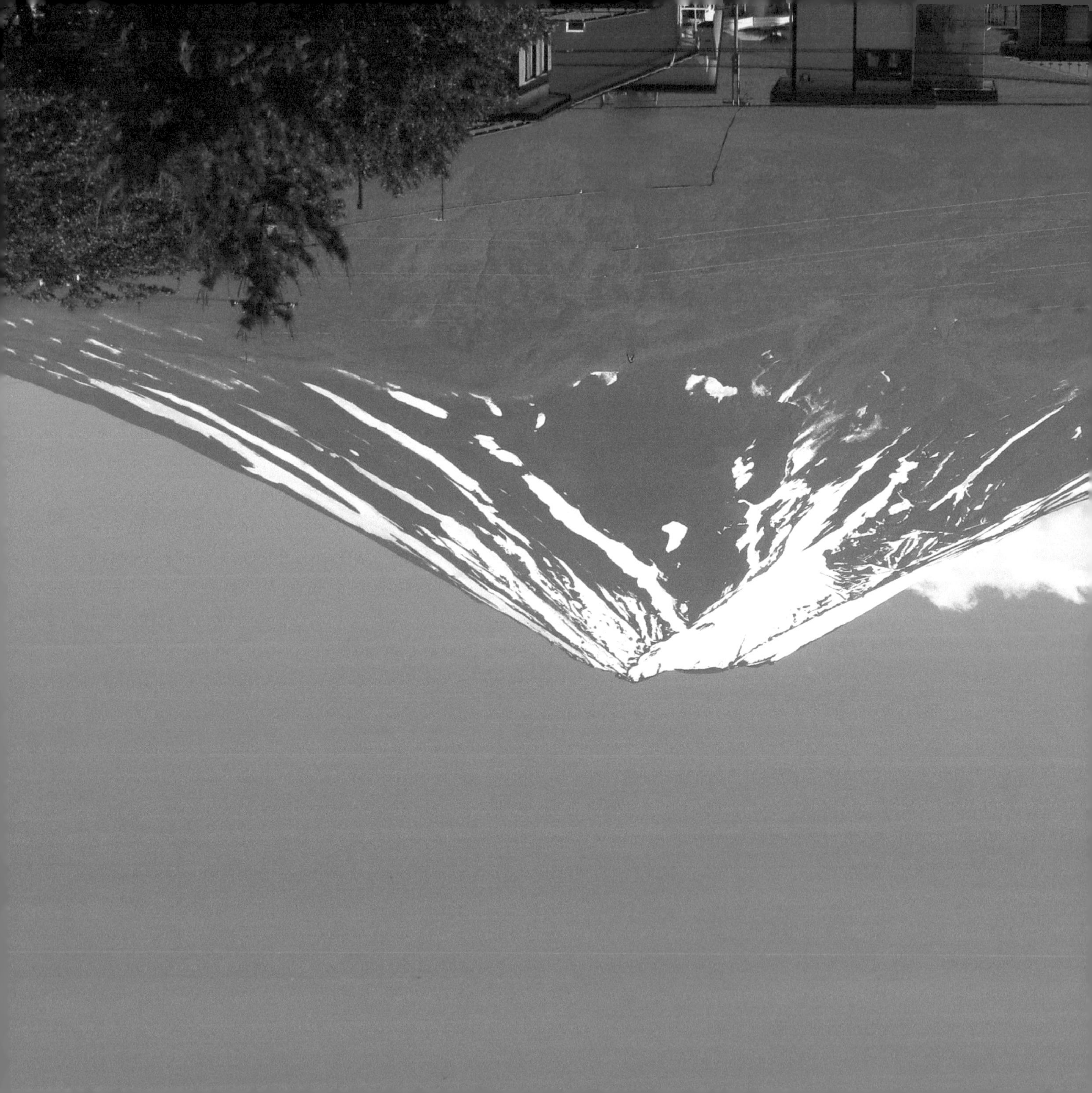

# July 2016

| Sun | Mon | Tue | Wed | Thu | Fri | Sat |
|---|---|---|---|---|---|---|
| 26 | 27 | 28 | 29 | 30 | 1 | 2 |
| 3 | 4<br>Independence Day | 5 | 6 | 7 | 8 | 9 |
| 10 | 11 | 12 | 13 | 14 | 15 | 16 |
| 17 | 18 | ☺ | 20 | 21 | 22 | 23 |
| 24 | 25 | 26 | 27 | 28 | 29 | 30 |
| 31 | 1 | 2 | 3 | 4 | 5 | 6 |

Mt. Fuji, Taken from Kawaguchi Lake Station.  Yamanashi Prefecture, Japan.

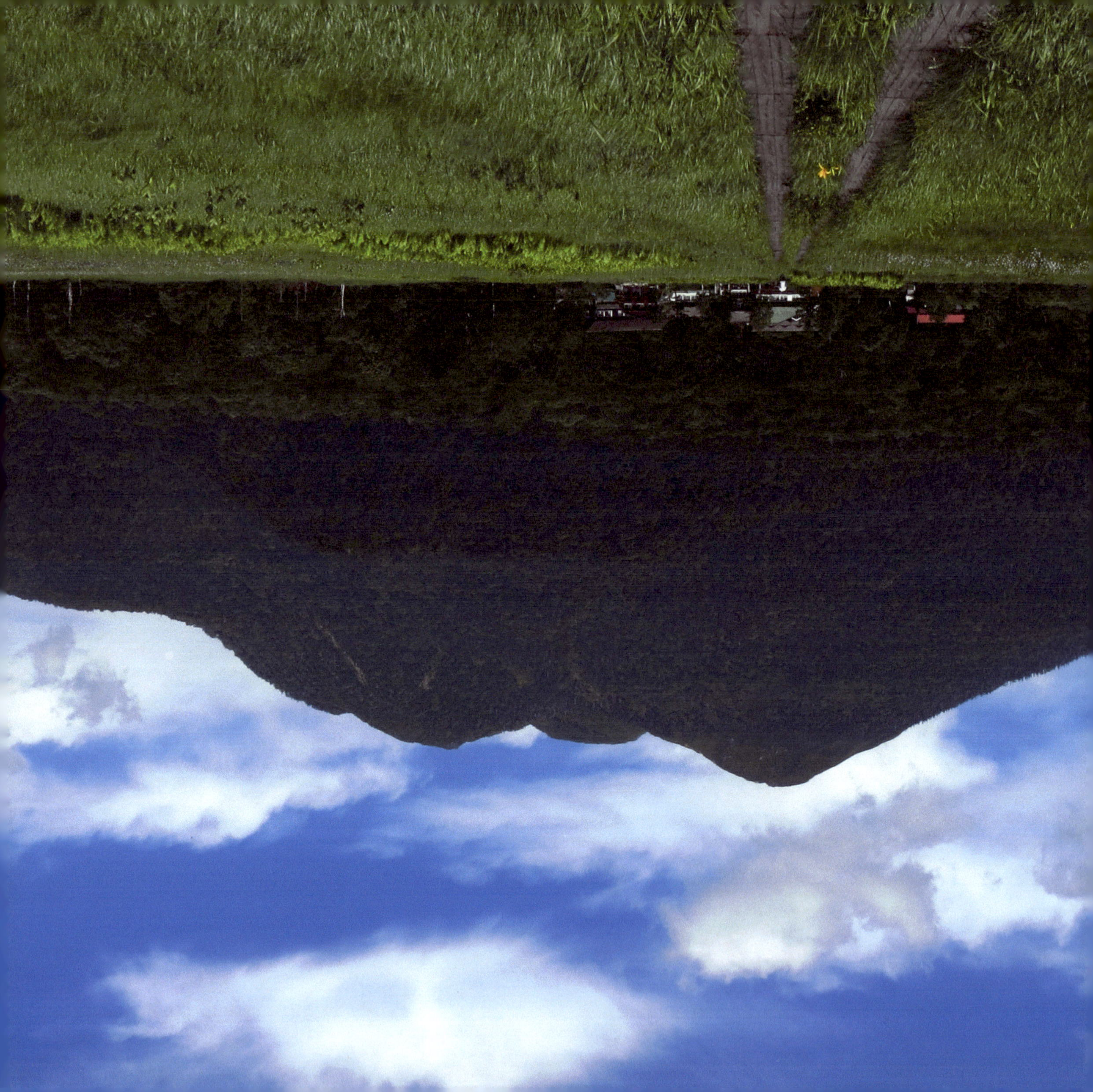

# August 2016

| Sun | Mon | Tue | Wed | Thu | Fri | Sat |
|---|---|---|---|---|---|---|
| 31 | 1 | 2 | 3 | 4 | 5 | 6 |
| 7 | 8 | 9 | 10 | 11 | 12 | 13 |
| 14 | 15 | 16 | 17 | ☺ | 19 | 20 |
| 21 | 22 | 23 | 24 | 25 | 26 | 27 |
| 28 | 29 | 30 | 31 | 1 | 2 | 3 |

Mt. Hiuchigatake & Oze Marsh, Oze National Park.  Fukushima Prefecture, Japan.

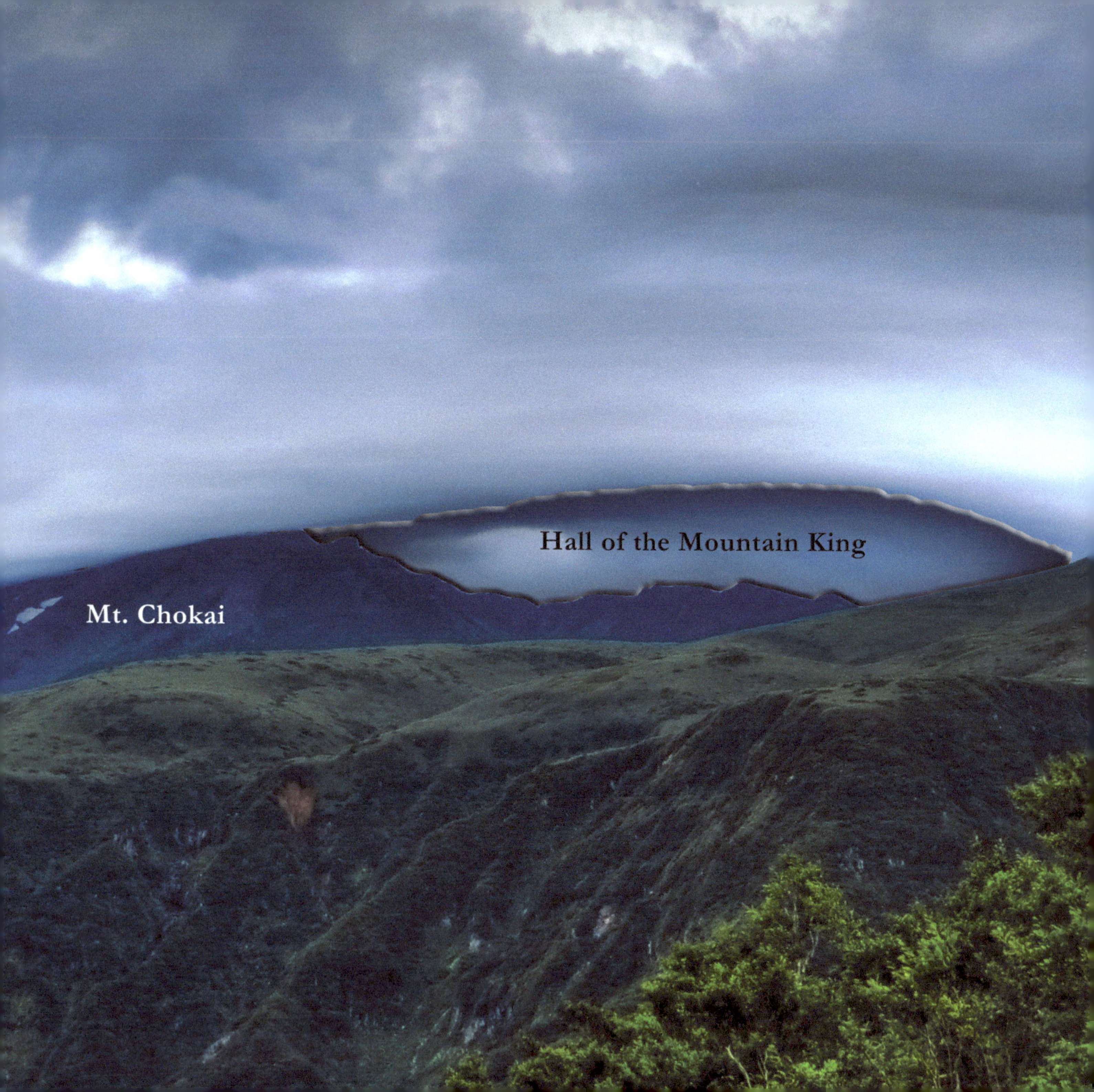

Mt. Chokai
Hall of the Mountain King

# September 2016

| Sun | Mon | Tue | Wed | Thu | Fri | Sat |
|---|---|---|---|---|---|---|
| 28 | 29 | 30 | 31 | 1 | 2 | 3 |
| 4 | 5<br>Labor Day | 6 | 7 | 8 | 9 | 10 |
| 11 | 12 | 13 | 14 | 15 | ☺ | 17 |
| 18 | 19 | 20 | 21 | 22<br>14:21 GMT<br>Autumnal Equinox | 23 | 24 |
| 25 | 26 | 27 | 28 | 29 | 30 | 1 |

Mt. Chokai & Interesting Cloud Phenomenon.  Yamagata/Akita Prefectures, Japan.

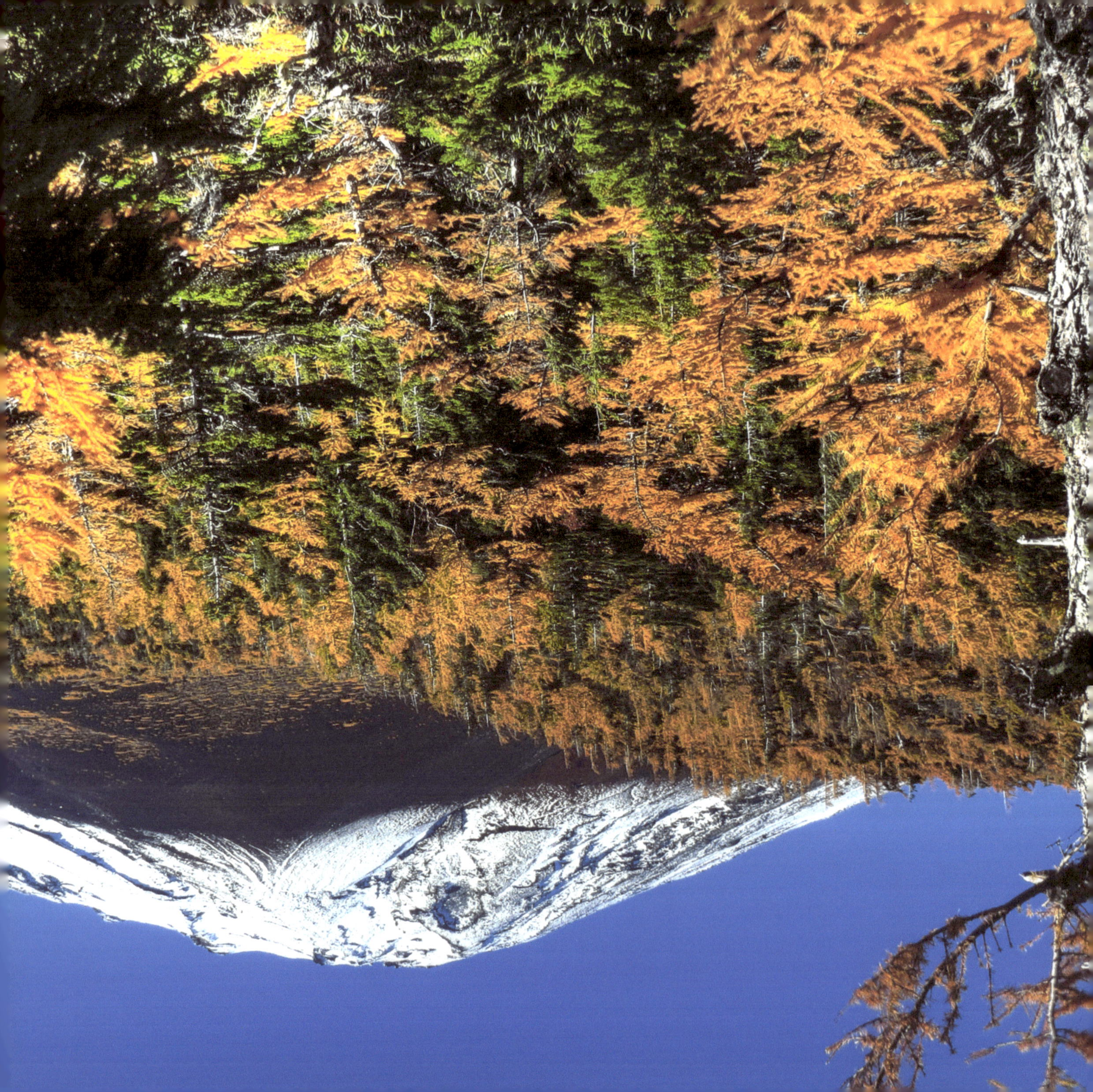

# October 2016

| Sun | Mon | Tue | Wed | Thu | Fri | Sat |
|---|---|---|---|---|---|---|
| 25 | 26 | 27 | 28 | 29 | 30 | 1 |
| 2 | 3 | 4 | 5 | 6 | 7 | 8 |
| 9 | 10<br>Columbus Day | 11 | 12 | 13 | 14 | 15 |
| 16 | 17 | 18 | 19 | 20 | 21 | 22 |
| 23 | 24 | 25 | 26 | 27 | 28 | 29 |
| 30 | 31<br>Halloween | 1 | 2 | 3 | 4 | 5 |

Mt. Fuji from the Okuniwa Area.  Yamanashi Prefecture, Japan.

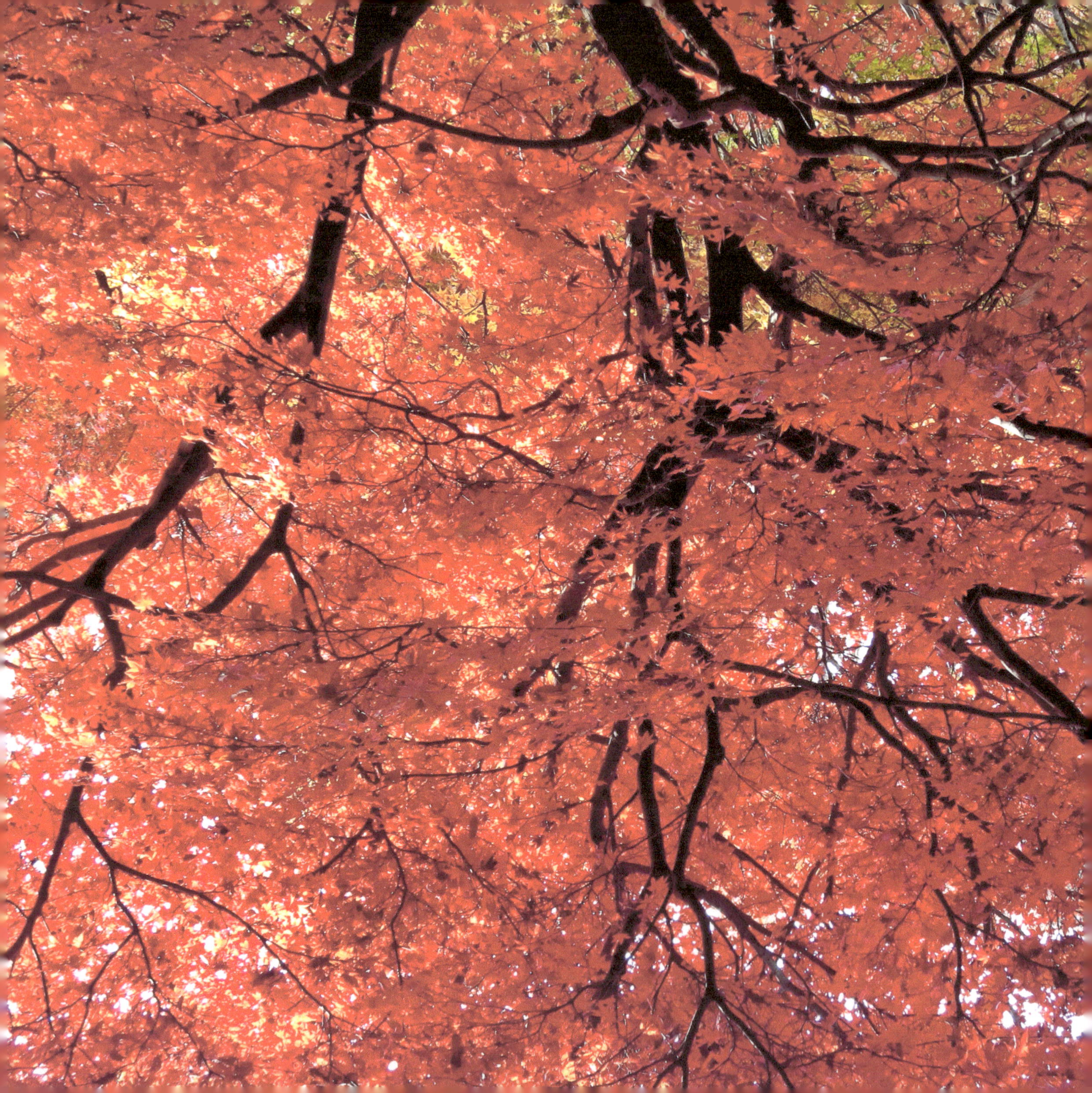

# November 2016

| Sun | Mon | Tue | Wed | Thu | Fri | Sat |
|---|---|---|---|---|---|---|
| 30 | 31 | 1 | 2 | 3 | 4 | 5 |
| 6<br>**Daylight Saving Time End (02:00)** | 7 | 8 | 9 | 10 | 11<br>**Veteran's Day** | 12 |
| 13 | ☻ | 15 | 16 | 17 | 18 | 19 |
| 20 | 21 | 22 | 23 | 24<br>**Thanksgiving Day** | 25 | 26 |
| 27 | 28 | 29 | 30 | 1 | 2 | 3 |

A Beautiful Red Maple at Jindai Botanical Garden.  Tokyo, Japan.

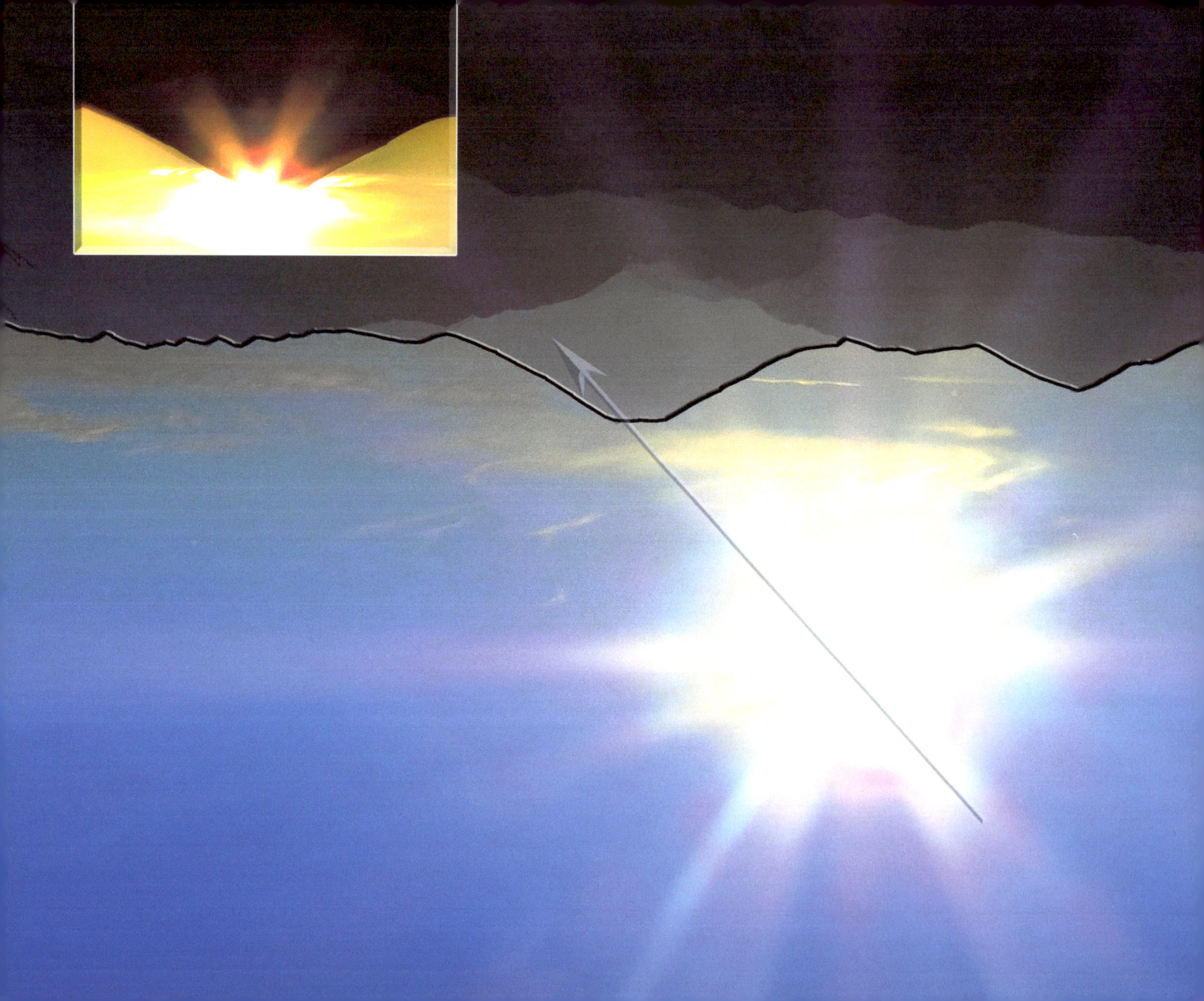

# December 2016

| Sun | Mon | Tue | Wed | Thu | Fri | Sat |
|---|---|---|---|---|---|---|
| 27 | 28 | 29 | 30 | 1 | 2 | 3 |
| 4 | 5 | 6 | 7 | 8 | 9 | 10 |
| 11 | 12 | 13 | 14 | 15 | 16 | 17 |
| 18 | 19 | 20 | 21<br>**10:44 GMT**<br>**Winter Solstice** | 22 | 23 | 24<br>**Christmas Eve** |
| 25<br>**Christmas Day** | 26<br>**Christmas Day observed** | 27 | 28 | 29 | 30 | 31<br>**New Year's Eve** |

"Diamond Fuji" – The Day the Sun Sets Behind Mt. Fuji – Taken at Summit of Mt. Takao.  Tokyo, Japan.
Gray arrow shows path of sun.  Inset photo taken 22 minutes after main photo.

# 2016 Phases of the Moon

Universal Time (GMT)

| | New Moon | | | | First Quarter | | | | Full Moon | | | | Last Quarter | | |
|---|---|---|---|---|---|---|---|---|---|---|---|---|---|---|---|
| | d | h | m | | d | h | m | | d | h | m | | d | h | m |
| -- | -- | -- | -- | -- | -- | -- | -- | -- | -- | -- | -- | JAN | 02 | 05 | 30 |
| JAN | 10 | 01 | 30 | JAN | 16 | 23 | 26 | JAN | 24 | 01 | 46 | FEB | 01 | 03 | 28 |
| FEB | 08 | 14 | 39 | FEB | 15 | 07 | 46 | FEB | 22 | 18 | 20 | MAR | 01 | 23 | 11 |
| MAR | 09 | 01 | 54 | MAR | 15 | 17 | 03 | MAR | 23 | 12 | 01 | MAR | 31 | 15 | 17 |
| APR | 07 | 11 | 24 | APR | 14 | 03 | 59 | APR | 22 | 05 | 24 | APR | 30 | 03 | 29 |
| MAY | 06 | 19 | 29 | MAY | 13 | 17 | 02 | MAY | 21 | 21 | 14 | MAY | 29 | 12 | 12 |
| JUN | 05 | 03 | 00 | JUN | 12 | 08 | 10 | JUN | 20 | 11 | 02 | JUN | 27 | 18 | 19 |
| JUL | 04 | 11 | 01 | JUL | 12 | 00 | 52 | JUL | 19 | 22 | 56 | JUL | 26 | 23 | 00 |
| AUG | 02 | 20 | 44 | AUG | 10 | 18 | 21 | AUG | 18 | 09 | 26 | AUG | 25 | 03 | 41 |
| SEP | 01 | 09 | 03 | SEP | 09 | 11 | 49 | SEP | 16 | 19 | 05 | SEP | 23 | 09 | 56 |
| OCT | 01 | 00 | 11 | OCT | 09 | 04 | 33 | OCT | 16 | 04 | 23 | OCT | 22 | 19 | 14 |
| OCT | 30 | 17 | 38 | NOV | 02 | 19 | 51 | NOV | 14 | 13 | 52 | NOV | 21 | 08 | 33 |
| NOV | 29 | 12 | 18 | DEC | 07 | 09 | 03 | DEC | 14 | 00 | 05 | DEC | 21 | 01 | 56 |
| DEC | 29 | 06 | 53 | -- | -- | -- | -- | -- | -- | -- | -- | -- | -- | -- | -- |

# Earth's Seasons – 2016

Universal Time (GMT)

| | | d | h | | | d | h | m | | d | h | m |
|---|---|---|---|---|---|---|---|---|---|---|---|---|
| Perihelion | Jan | 02 | 23 | Equinoxes | Mar | 20 | 04 | 30 | Sept | 22 | 14 | 21 |
| Aphelion | July | 04 | 16 | Solstices | June | 20 | 22 | 34 | Dec | 21 | 10 | 44 |

If you enjoyed the photographs shown in this calendar then please be sure to check out our website. It can be found at http://danwiz.com. As long as he is alive he hopes to be able to maintain it.

Kazuya's blog can be found at: http://studiesofplantsandwildlife.blogspot.com  or alternately, http://www2.blogger.com/profile/02622643778290337101.